NATIONAL GEOGRAPHIC

**EXPLORE OUR WORLD**

STUDENT BOOK **3**

**SERIES EDITORS**
JoAnn (Jodi) Crandall
Joan Kang Shin

**AUTHORS**
Rob Sved
Gabrielle Pritchard

T0349598

NATIONAL GEOGRAPHIC LEARNING | CENGAGE Learning·

Australia • Brazil • Japan • Korea • Mexico • Singapore • Spain • United Kingdom • United States

# Welcome to Our Class.

**1** **Look, listen, and say.** TR: 2

How do you say *borrador* in English?

It's an *eraser*.

How do you spell *scissors?*

s-c-i-s-s-o-r-s

Could you repeat that, please?

Sure, s-c-i-s-s-o-r-s.

I don't understand. Can you help me, please?

Yes, sure.

What's the difference between *next to* and *in front of?*

I can show you.

# Seasons and months

**2** **Look, listen, and say.** TR: 3

spring

summer

fall

winter

**3** **Look and listen.** Point and say. TR: 4

**4** **Look, listen, and say.** TR: 5

| January | February | March | April |
| May | June | July | August |
| September | October | November | December |

It's December. It's cold here.

It's December, but it's hot here.

**5** **Look, listen, and say.** TR: 6

| 20 | 21 | 22 | 23 | 24 |
|---|---|---|---|---|
| twenty | twenty-one | twenty-two | twenty-three | twenty-four |

| 25 | 26 | 27 | 28 | 29 |
|---|---|---|---|---|
| twenty-five | twenty-six | twenty-seven | twenty-eight | twenty-nine |

| 30 | 40 | 50 | 60 | 70 |
|---|---|---|---|---|
| thirty | forty | fifty | sixty | seventy |

| 80 | 90 | 100 | 101 | 102 |
|---|---|---|---|---|
| eighty | ninety | one hundred | one hundred and one | one hundred and two |

**200**
two hundred

| 1,000 | 1,000,000 | 1,000,000,000 |
|---|---|---|
| one thousand | one million | one billion |

| **+** | **–** | **=** |
|---|---|---|
| plus | minus | equals |

**6** **Work with a partner.** Listen. Do the math together. Listen to check your answers. TR: 7

| | | |
|---|---|---|
| 24 + 2 = | 80 + 9 = | 300 – 50 = |
| 100 + 10 = | 35 + 5 = | 1,000 + 1,000 = |
| 60 + 20 = | 40 – 30 = | 99 – 9 = |

Twenty plus five equals . . .

Twenty-five!

**7** **Look, listen, and say.** TR: 8

| 1st | 2nd | 3rd | 4th | 5th |
|-----|-----|-----|-----|-----|
| **first** | **second** | **third** | **fourth** | **fifth** |

| | | | |
|---|---|---|---|
| 6th **sixth** | 10th **tenth** | 14th **fourteenth** | 18th **eighteenth** |
| 7th **seventh** | 11th **eleventh** | 15th **fifteenth** | 19th **nineteenth** |
| 8th **eighth** | 12th **twelfth** | 16th **sixteenth** | 20th **twentieth** |
| 9th **ninth** | 13th **thirteenth** | 17th **seventeenth** | 21st **twenty-first** |

**8** **Ask and answer.**

When's your birthday?

September 15th.

5

## 9 Look, listen, and say. TR: 9

The kite is **mine**.

The coat is **yours**.

The ball is **his**.

The bat is **hers**.

The grapes are **ours**.

The pencils are **yours**.

The game is **theirs**.

## 10 Look around your classroom. Ask and answer.

Whose pencil is this?

It's yours.

**11** **Read and write.**

me

you

him

her

it

us

you

them

1. John! Jenny! I have some lunch for _____.

2. Hey, Dad. Can I help _____?

3. Thanks, Jenny. Where's your brother? I can't see _____.

4. Mom is over there. Maybe he's with _____.

5. Go get _____. It's time to eat!

6. I love chicken sandwiches! Give _____ that big one!

7. Dad, we want to play soccer. Do you want to come with

_____?

8. Okay, where's the ball? Oh, I see _____!

# Unit 1

# The World of Work

**Look and check.**

The women are

◯ in a swimming pool.

◯ in the ocean.

They are

◯ working.

◯ on vacation.

Sylvia Earle working outside an underwater habitat

**1** **Listen and say.** TR: 10

**2** **Listen, point, and say.** TR: 11

a farmer

a vet

a scientist

a doctor

a bus driver

a police officer

a nurse

a firefighter

a chef

He's wearing a yellow hat.

**3** **Work with a partner.**
Ask and answer.

Is he a firefighter?

| What **does** your father **do?** | He's a chef. |
| Where does your father work? | He **works** in a restaurant. |

**4** **Play a game.** Spin, ask, and answer. Play with a partner.

**5** **Work with a partner.** Talk about what these people do.

**6** **Listen and say.** Look and write. TR: 13

an inventor

a rock star

an artist

a movie star

a soccer player

1. This person plays a sport. _She's a soccer player._ _____

2. This person draws and paints pictures. _____

3. This person sings to lots of people. _____

4. This person makes new things. _____

5. This person is in the movies. _____

**7** **Listen and stick.** TR: 14

| 1 | 2 | 3 | 4 | 5 |
|---|---|---|---|---|

What **do** you **want to be** one day? | I **want to be** a movie star.
What **does** your brother **want to be?** | He **wants to be** a doctor.

**8** **Read and write.**

1. She loves animals. What does she want to be?

_____

2. She plays guitar in a band. What does she want to be?

_____

3. She likes cooking. What does she want to be?

_____

4. He loves to draw and paint. What does he want to be?

_____

**9** **Play a game.** Cut out the cube and the cards on page 97.
Play in groups of six.

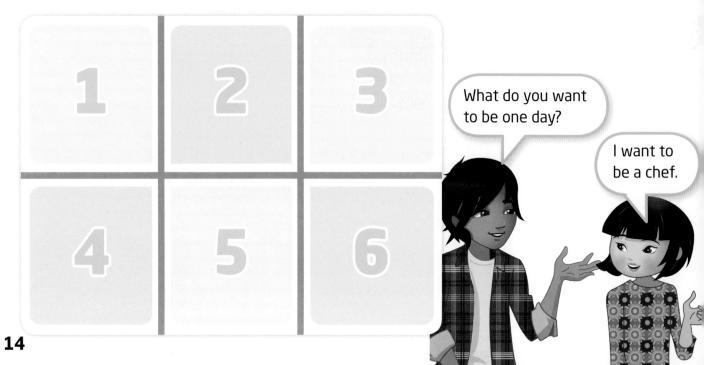

| 1 | 2 | 3 |
| 4 | 5 | 6 |

What do you want to be one day?

I want to be a chef.

14

**10** **Listen.** Read and sing. TR: 16

# Work

*What does your father do?*
*What does your mother do?*
*What does your brother do?*
*What do they do?*

**THE SOUNDS OF ENGLISH** TR: 17

**f**armer

**11** **Listen and say.**

1. farmer       firefighter

2. father       fish

3. sofa         chef

# Wonderful Work!

Annie Griffiths is a photographer. She travels all over the world for her work. She takes photographs of people at work and people having fun. She also takes photos of cute animals and some very scary animals. Annie wants all her photos to tell a story. She wants people to think about them.

**The first photo of a person is from Paris in 1838.**

Victoria Falls, Zambia

**1861** First color photograph

**1814** First photograph

**1999** First camera and video phone

**1984** First digital camera

**13** **Work with a partner.** Talk. Today you are a photographer. What do you want to photograph?

I want to take pictures of the mountains.

I want to take a picture of my family.

# Work hard.

Work hard and enjoy your work.

## Do you work hard?
## What do you do?

NATIONAL GEOGRAPHIC

A woman picks tea leaves in Yunnan Province, China.

# Unit 2
# Let's Eat!

**Look and circle.**

This animal is    small.    big.

It is    drinking.    eating.

Gecko, Hawaii

bread

tomatoes

corn

potatoes

20

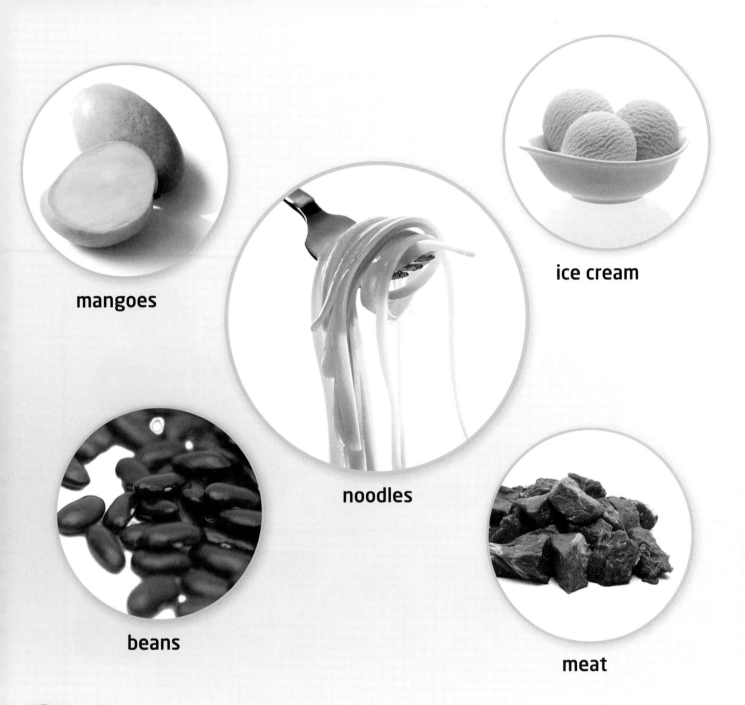

mangoes

noodles

ice cream

beans

meat

**3** **Work with a partner.** Point. Ask and answer.

Do you like apples and mangoes?

I like apples, but I don't like mangoes.

21

| | |
|---|---|
| Are there **any** tomatoes? | No, there aren't **any** tomatoes. |
| Are there **any** potatoes? | Yes, there are. |
| Is there **any** bread? | No, there isn't **any** bread. |
| Is there **any** milk? | Yes, there is. |

**4** **Play a game.** What's the same? Play with a partner.

Is there any milk?

No, there isn't. Are there any potatoes?

**5** **Listen and say.** Look and write the letter. TR: 22

snacks

grapes

chips

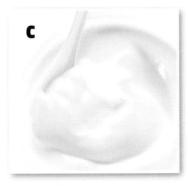
yogurt

nuts

cheese

1. I eat chips after school. _____

2. My favorite snack is cheese. _____

3. I like yogurt for breakfast. _____

4. I don't like nuts. _____

5. Red grapes are delicious! _____

**6** **Work with a partner.** Talk. Guess and stick.

This is a boy.

Is he eating grapes?

No, he isn't.

Is he eating nuts?

Yes, he is!

1  2  3  4  5

| | |
|---|---|
| **May** I have some chips, please? | Not right now. Dinner is at 7:00. |
| **May** we have some noodles, please? | Yes. Sure. |

**7** **Look.** Write questions.

_____

_____

_____

_____

**8** **Play a game.** Cut out the gameboard and the pictures on page 99. Glue. Play with a partner.

B2. May I have some chips, please?

Sorry. I don't have any chips. C1. May I have some lemonade, please?

24

**9** **Listen.** Read and sing. TR: 24

# Let's Eat!

*Let's eat! Do you like chicken?*
*Let's eat! Do you like bread?*
*Let's eat! Are there any carrots?*
*Let's eat!*

*Are there any mangoes?*
*Is there any cheese?*
*Is there any yogurt?*
*May I have some, please?*

**THE SOUNDS OF ENGLISH** TR: 25

**m**ango

**10** **Listen and say.**

1. mango   meat

2. marker   map

3. grandmother   room

25

**11** **Listen and read.** TR: 26

# Super Snacks!

People all over the world eat snacks such as fruit, chips, nuts, and candy. What other snacks do people enjoy?

Do you like fried butter or garlic ice cream? What about ice cream with fish? You can eat these snacks in some parts of North America.

In some countries in Latin America, you can eat insects such as ants, termites, and grasshoppers. In some parts of Asia, you can eat fried silkworms, water bugs, and scorpions on sticks.

In Australia, people like to eat honey ants. In other places, lollipops with insects are popular.

It's snack time! How about a sweet cricket, worm, or scorpion lollipop?

**12** **Talk with a partner.** Which of these snacks do you want to try?

Cats can't taste candy.

# Eat good food.

Eat fruits and vegetables. Have good snacks. Drink water every day.

Koala

## What good things do you eat? What good things do you drink?

NATIONAL GEOGRAPHIC

# A Helping Hand

**Look and check.**

This is a baby

○ zebra.

○ tiger.

The woman is

○ smiling.

○ crying.

Zookeeper feeds tiger cub,
Gianyar, Indonesia

**1** **Listen and read.** TR: 27

**2** **Listen and say.** TR: 28

We care for each other and we care for animals. We help in many different ways.

help

carry

hug

teach

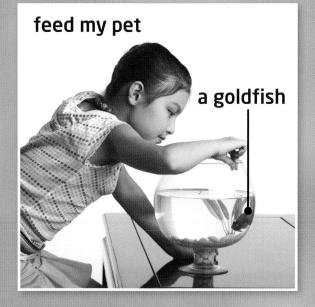

feed my pet

a goldfish

protect

take care of my pet

a hamster

**3** **Work with a partner.**
Ask and answer.

What do you like to do?

I like to take care of my goldfish.

31

What does she do **before** breakfast?　She gets dressed **before** breakfast.
What does he do **after** school?　He feeds his bird **after** school.

**4** **Play a game.** Play with a partner.

blue frame = before school
green frame = after school

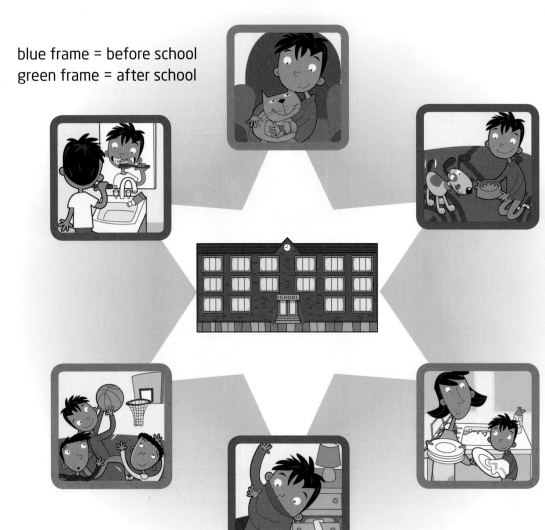

What does he do before school?

He brushes his teeth before school.

**5** **Listen and say.** Check **T** for *True* and **F** for *False*. TR: 30

take a shower

make my bed

come home

have a snack

do my homework

1. She makes her bed at eight fifteen. (T) (F)

2. She has a snack at four forty-five. (T) (F)

3. She does her homework at five o'clock. (T) (F)

4. She takes a shower at six thirty. (T) (F)

5. She comes home at three twenty-five. (T) (F)

**6** **Stick and write times.**
Work with a partner.

What time do you take a shower?

I take a shower at 7:45.

: _____    : _____    : _____    : _____    : _____

33

I **never** eat lunch at 12:30.

I **usually** eat lunch at 12:30.

I **sometimes** eat lunch at 12:30.

I **always** eat lunch at 12:30.

**7** **Read and write.**

never ○○○  sometimes ●○○
usually ●●○  always ●●●

| | 🚿 8:15 | ⚽ 6:30 | 🧹 6:30 | 🛏️ 8:45 |
|---|---|---|---|---|
| Meena | ●○○ | ○○○ | ●●○ | ●●● |
| Tom | ●●● | ●○○ | ○○○ | ●●○ |

1. **Meena**  I _____*never*_____ play soccer at 6:30.

2. **Tom**  I _____ take a shower at 8:15.

3. **Meena**  I _____ help at home at 6:30.

4. **Tom**  I _____ go to bed at 8:45.

5. **Meena**  I _____ take a shower at 8:15.

**8** **Play a game.** Cut out the game board and cards on page 101. Play with a partner.

I usually make my bed in the morning.

I always make my bed in the morning.

So we're different.

**Listen.** Read and sing. TR: 32

# Taking Care

*I love taking care of my pets.*
*I love taking care of my family.*
*I love taking care of them all.*
*I'm happy that there are so many!*

**THE SOUNDS OF ENGLISH** TR: 33

h**o**me

**10** **Listen and say.**

1. home        goldfish

2. cold         coat

3. stove        yellow

# My Mom, the Airplane

There are not many whooping cranes in the world. People have to protect these birds and help them live safely. Luckily, there are some special places in North America where people protect the whooping crane's eggs. They also take care of the baby cranes.

These baby cranes have no mothers to teach them, so they follow a scientist who wears a crane suit. Then they learn to follow a small airplane. They listen to the airplane, too. Soon they're happy to fly with the airplane—they think the airplane is their mother!

whooping crane

All birds come from dinosaurs!

**12** **Compare.** Work with a partner.

How are airplanes and birds alike?

How are birds and dinosaurs alike?

Wingspans

**244 cm** (8 ft.)

**46 cm** (1.5 ft.)

parrot

whooping crane

# Take care of others.

Sometimes other people need your help. Be caring.

## How can you take care of others?

**NATIONAL GEOGRAPHIC**

Emperor penguin with chick

# My Place in the World

**Look and check.**

I can see

◯ North America.

◯ South America.

◯ Asia.

## 1 Listen and read. TR: 35

## 2 Listen and say. TR: 36

You can find the places in these photos in most cities. Do you have these places where you live?

a hospital

a bakery

a museum

a restaurant

a supermarket

a park

a train station

a movie theater

a toy store

a police station

**3** **Work with a partner.** Describe and guess.
Use these words.

| a doctor | a toy car | food | movies |
|----------|-----------|------|--------|
| paintings | bread | a police officer | |

You can see paintings here.

It's a museum!

41

**Can** you **help** me?    Sure. How **can** I **help**?

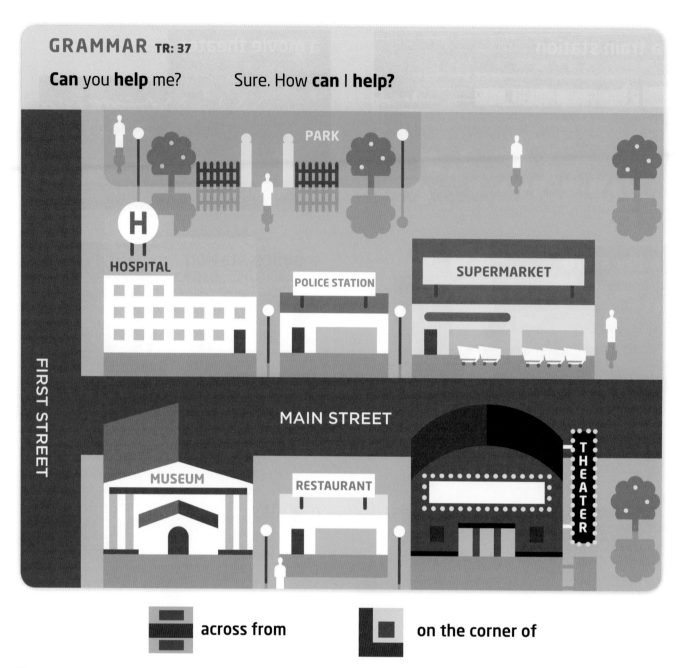

across from    on the corner of

4 **Work with a partner.** Ask and answer.

Can you help me?

Sure. How can I help?

Where's the supermarket?

It's next to the police station and across from the theater.

## 5 Listen and say.
### Read and write. TR: 38

a library

a swimming pool

a zoo

a mall

a stadium

1. Min wants to go to the _____.
   She loves the crocodiles and the monkeys.

2. Aziz wants to go to the _____.
   He likes to see his favorite soccer team.

3. Janica wants to go to the _____.
   She has a new bathing suit.

4. Mounira wants to go to the _____.
   She wants to buy some new clothes.

5. Leo wants to go the _____.
   He wants to read some books.

## 6 Listen and stick. TR: 39

| Monday | Tuesday | Wednesday | Thursday | Friday |
|--------|---------|-----------|----------|--------|
|        |         |           |          |        |

How can I get to the bakery?

Go straight ↑.
Turn left ← on Third Avenue.
Turn right → at the supermarket.

**7** **Look at the map below.** Follow and write.

1. How can I get to the _____? Turn left on Summer Street. Go straight. Turn right on Spring Street. It's next to the mall.

2. How _____? Go straight on Green Street. Turn left on Middle Street. It's on the corner of Middle Street and Second Avenue.

3. How _____? Go straight on Green Street. Turn right on Middle Street. Turn left on Black Street. It's next to the swimming pool.

4. How _____? Turn left on Summer Street. Turn right on Second Avenue. Go straight on to Sunny Street. It's next to the bookstore.

**8** **Play a game.** Cut out the cards on page 103. Play with a partner. Ask for directions. Take turns.

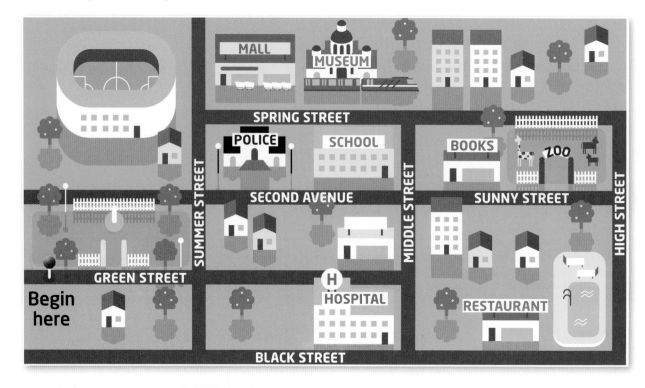

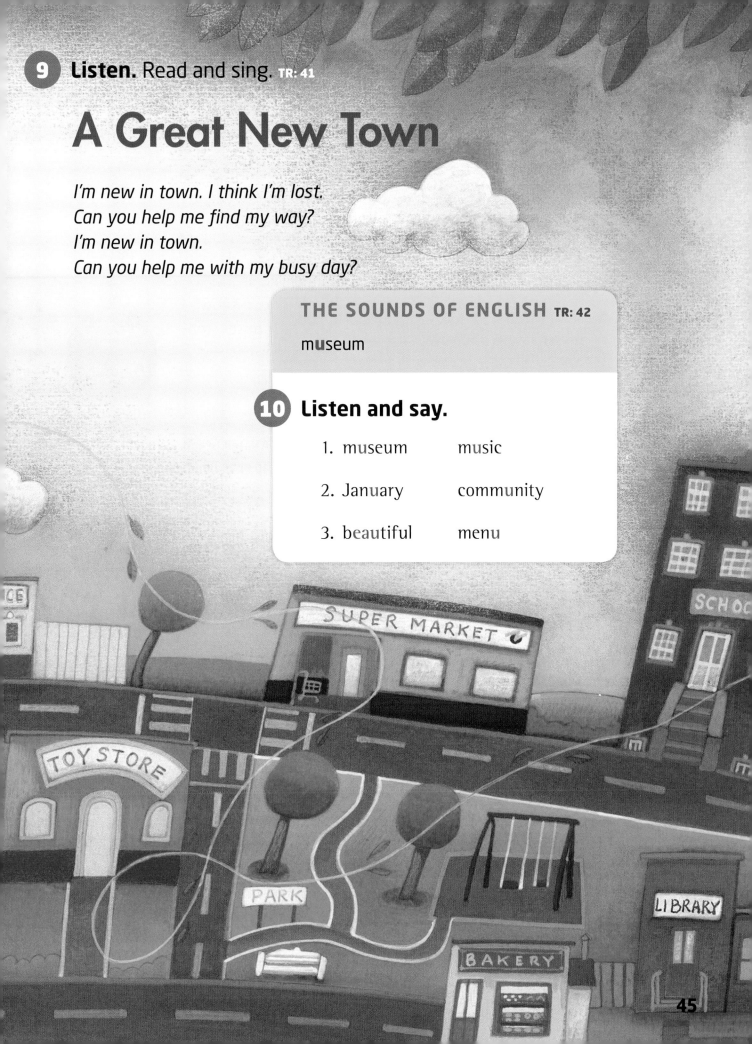

**9** **Listen.** Read and sing. TR: 41

# A Great New Town

*I'm new in town. I think I'm lost.*
*Can you help me find my way?*
*I'm new in town.*
*Can you help me with my busy day?*

**THE SOUNDS OF ENGLISH** TR: 42

m**u**seum

**10** **Listen and say.**

1. museum     music

2. January     community

3. beautiful    menu

## 11 **Listen and read.** TR: 43

# Eye in the Sky

Satellites are machines in space that circle Earth. They help us talk to people on the other side of the planet. They can also study the planet's weather.

This satellite is called GeoEye 1. It's the same size as a big car. It takes photos of our planet. These photos can show continents and oceans. They can show streets and houses, too!

681 km
(423 miles)

## 12 **Work with a partner.** Talk about your town. You can use a photo or map.

**Weird but true**
A satellite can see an open umbrella from space!

This is part of Asia, the biggest continent. Now we can see the countries clearly. Here we can see South Korea.

Now we can see one town. This is Pohang in South Korea. Look! Can you see the river?

# Explore your town.

It's fun to find new things and places to explore.

## How can you explore your town?

NATIONAL GEOGRAPHIC

Shanghai, China

# Review

**Start**

5:00 P.M.

**Finish**

Your pet is hungry. Go back two spaces!

7:20 A.M.

8:15 A.M.

You work hard.
Go forward
two spaces!

7:30 A.M.

**Work with a partner.** Use a coin.
Look. Ask and answer.

Tails! One space. What
do you do after school?

I play soccer with
my friends.

 **Heads =**
2 spaces

 **Tails =**
1 space

# Unit 5
# On the Move!

**Check T for *True* and F for *False*.**

The city

1. is very quiet.     **T** **F**

2. has a lot of cars.     **T** **F**

Taksim Square, Istanbul

## 1 **Listen and read.** TR: 44

## 2 **Listen and say.** TR: 45

Transportation helps us move around. We can travel in the sky, on water, or on land. Which is your favorite?

an airplane

a boat

a helicopter

a bus

a ship

the subway

a scooter

a scooter

a taxi

a motorcycle

**3** **Work with a partner.** Describe and guess.

It's in the sky.

Is it an airplane?

53

| | |
|---|---|
| I ride my scooter to school. | **I do, too.** |
| I take the bus to school. | **I don't.** I take the subway. |
| My brother rides his bike to school. | My brother **does, too.** |
| My sister takes the bus to school. | My sister **doesn't.** She walks. |

**4** **Play a game.** Play with a partner. Talk about you, your family, and your friends.

I sleep with my teddy bear.

My sister does, too.

## 5 Listen and say. Read and write. TR: 47

get on

uphill

downhill

get off

park

1. After school, I _____ my bike, and I ride home. I can ride home in fifteen minutes.

2. I sometimes go _____. I get tired, but at the top of the hill I can see the whole town!

3. I like to go _____, too. I go fast, but I'm careful.

4. When I get home, I _____ my bike and _____ it. I'm usually hungry, so I have a snack.

## 6 Listen and stick. TR: 48

| 1 | 2 | 3 | 4 | 5 |
|---|---|---|---|---|

My mother takes the bus to work, **but** my father takes the subway.

**7** **Look at the pictures and complete.**

1. The boy rides his scooter to school,

   _but the girl rides her bike to school._

2. The girl eats breakfast at eight o'clock,

   _____

3. The boy has a rabbit,

   _____

4. He wants to be a singer,

   _____

5. The girl has noodles for lunch,

   _____

**8** **Play a game.** Cut out the cards on page 105. Play with a partner. Make sentences about the cards. Find and keep pairs.

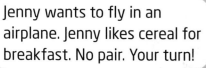

Jenny wants to fly in an airplane. Jenny likes cereal for breakfast. No pair. Your turn!

Pair! Jenny likes to play tennis on Saturdays, but Sam likes to play soccer on Saturdays.

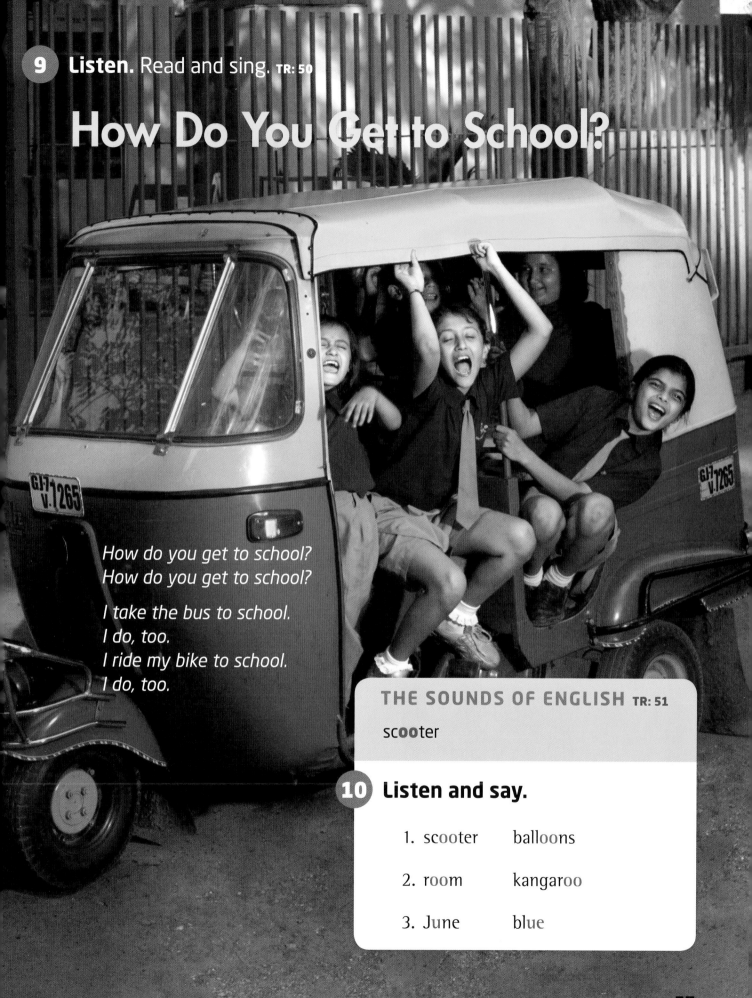

# How Do You Get to School?

How do you get to school?
How do you get to school?

I take the bus to school.
I do, too.
I ride my bike to school.
I do, too.

**THE SOUNDS OF ENGLISH** TR: 51

sc**oo**ter

10 **Listen and say.**

1. scooter    balloons

2. room       kangaroo

3. June       blue

57

# Hot Air Balloons

In October every year, there is an International Balloon Fiesta in Albuquerque, USA. About 600 colorful balloons are up in the sky at the same time. What fun!

How do hot air balloons fly? When the balloon is on the ground, people light gas to make a small fire. This heats the air in the balloon. Hot air always goes up. So, the balloon goes up slowly into the air. The pilot stands in the basket and lights the gas to go higher. The wind blows the balloon along.

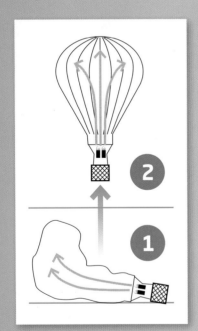

 The first passengers in a hot air balloon were a chicken, a duck, and a sheep!

**12** **Work with a partner.** Pretend you are in the sky in a balloon. What do you see? How do you feel? Talk.

# Be safe on the street.

Stop.
Look both ways.
Listen.

## How can we be safe on the street?

NATIONAL
GEOGRAPHIC

Busy intersection,
Macau, China

# Our Senses

**Look and check.**

This person is

&#9711; looking at the jellyfish.

&#9711; smelling the jellyfish.

Diver with jellyfish

We use our eyes, ears, nose, tongue, and skin to learn about the world around us.

ugly

beautiful

hard

soft

terrible

delicious

quiet

loud

**3** **Work with a partner.** Describe. Listen and guess.

| | | |
|---|---|---|
| a cake | an elephant | a flower |
| a rabbit | a rock | a fire truck |

It's small. It's soft. I think it's beautiful. What is it?

A rabbit!

The soup **smells** great.
The flowers **look** beautiful.
How **does** the chicken **taste?**

The music **sounds** terrible.
The baby rabbit **feels** soft.
It **tastes** delicious.

**4** **Play a game.** Play with a partner.
Describe what you see. Use your senses.

## 5 **Listen and say.** Read and write. TR: 56

sweet

salty

bitter

sour

spicy

1. This lemon isn't sweet. It's _____.

2. I don't like honey. I don't like _____ things.

3. These potato chips have a lot of salt. They're very _____.

4. I don't like the taste of coffee. It's very _____.

5. I like peppers. They're really _____.

## 6 **Listen and stick.** Work with a partner. Check your answers. TR: 57

Number 1 is spicy.

Yes. It's a pepper.

| 1 | 2 | 3 | 4 | 5 |
| --- | --- | --- | --- | --- |

| | |
|---|---|
| How is the ice cream? | It's delicious! |
| How **was** the ice cream? | It **was** delicious. More, please! |
| How **were** the cookies? | They **were** great. Can I have one more, please? |

**7** **Read and write.**

1. That ice cream _____ delicious. I want more!

2. The music _____ loud, but now it's quiet.

3. The flowers _____ beautiful before. They are ugly now.

4. Good job! That song _____ beautiful.

5. Those grapes _____ good. Are there any more?

**8** **Play a game.** Make the wheels on page 107.
Spin and make sentences. Play with a partner.

*Flowers, were.* The flowers were beautiful, but now they aren't.

Good job. My turn. *Music, are.* No match!

**9** **Listen.** Read and sing. TR: 59

# Our Senses

*How does the cake taste?*
*It tastes sweet.*
*How does a kitten feel?*
*It feels soft.*

*Let's count our senses. 1, 2, 3, 4, 5!*
*Listen. Look. Feel. Taste. Smell.*
*It's great to be alive!*

**THE SOUNDS OF ENGLISH** TR: 60

**s**oft

**10** **Listen and say.**

| | |
|---|---|
| 1. soft | salty |
| 2. subway | sister |
| 3. eraser | pants |

Polar bear mom with cubs,
Manitoba, Canada

## 11 **Listen and read.** TR: 61

# Amazing Animal Senses

Many animals see, hear, smell, taste, and touch in a different way from humans. Do you walk on your dinner to taste it? Well, a butterfly does—it tastes with its feet!

People use their fingers to touch. Seals use their whiskers. They can feel fish through the water 180 meters (590 feet) away.

Spiders don't have ears. They hear using hundreds of small hairs on their legs. Bears can smell things that are 32 kilometers (20 miles) away.

Chameleons can see very well. One eye looks up, and the other eye looks down. Chameleons can see all around them!

whisker

red-tailed hawk

person

mouse

## 12 **Work with a partner.** Talk about other animals you know.

I think dogs can hear very well.

I know bats can't see very well.

**weird but true**

A worm can taste with its whole body.

# Enjoy the world through your senses.

Take time to enjoy the world around you. Use your senses.

## How do your senses tell you about the world around you?

NATIONAL GEOGRAPHIC

**Iguazu Falls, Argentina and Brazil**

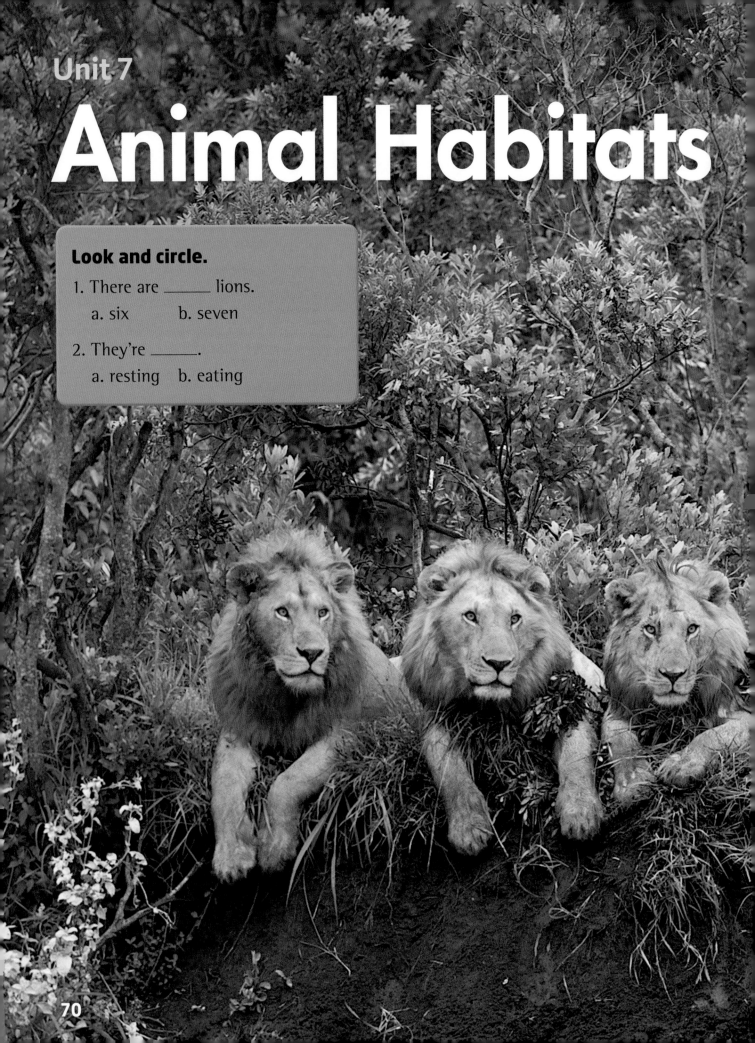

# Animal Habitats

**Look and circle.**

1. There are _____ lions.
   a. six          b. seven

2. They're _____.
   a. resting    b. eating

Lions resting, Tanzania

## 1 Listen and read. TR: 62

## 2 Listen and say. TR: 63

We all need a place to live. We live in houses or apartments. Animals and plants have a place to live, too. This place is called their habitat.

a forest

ice

a desert

a hive

Tenere Desert, Niger

a cave

mud

a rain forest

an island

a nest

snow

**3** **Work with a partner.** Ask and answer.

Where do camels live?

They live in the desert.

**Why** does a lion have sharp claws? **Because** it needs to catch its food.
**Why** are kangaroos so cool? **Because** they can jump so far!
**Why** don't you like penguins? **Because** they look silly, and they can't fly!

**4** **Play a game.** Play with a partner. Use a coin and draw lines.

 Heads = draw 1 line     Tails = draw 2 lines

Why does a polar bear cover its black nose?

Why do crocodiles have sharp teeth?

Why do leopards have spots?

Because it needs to see at night.

Because it wants to hide in the snow.

Because they eat meat.

Because they need to hide up in the trees.

Why does an owl have big eyes?

Because it can't fly, and it needs to run fast.

Why does an ostrich have long legs?

**5** **Listen and say.** Write the animals in the correct groups. TR: 65

a tongue

fur

horns

a pouch

wings

| cat | ~~parrot~~ | polar bear | penguin | cow |
| duck | rabbit | kangaroo | butterfly | goat |

| pouch | fur | wings | horns |
|-------|-----|-------|-------|
|       |     | parrot |      |
|       |     |       |       |

**6** **Work with a partner.** Guess and stick.

This animal is big and white. It lives in the snow. It has sharp claws.

It's a polar bear!

1   2   3   4   5

75

Giraffes use their long tongues **to clean** their ears.
Goats use their horns **to fight.**

**7** **Read and match.**

1. Cats use their tongues

2. Kangaroos use their pouches

3. Elephants use their long trunks

4. Tigers use their sharp teeth

5. Penguins use their wings

a. to carry their babies.

b. to eat meat.

c. to clean their fur.

d. to swim in the ocean.

e. to shower.

**8** **Play a game.** Cut out the cubes on page 109. Work with a partner. Make sentences.

Dogs use their trunks to drink water.

That's not true! Elephants use their trunks to drink water! Dogs don't have trunks!

**9** **Listen.** Read and sing. TR: 67

# Why? Because!

*I want to know why.*
*I want to know why.*
*Why?*
*Because I want to know why!*

**THE SOUNDS OF ENGLISH** TR: 68

p**ou**ch

**10** **Listen and say.**

1. pouch     house

2. bounce     cloud

3. brown     cow

# Amazing Rain Forests

Rain forests are warm, wet forests. A rain forest has four parts.

### Emergent
In this part, you can see the tops of very tall trees. They can be 60 meters (200 feet) tall! Many birds, butterflies, and other insects live here.

### Canopy
In this part of the forest, the trees have many leaves. Birds, spiders, tree frogs, monkeys, and snakes live here.

### Understory
In this part of the forest, it is dark, wet, and cool. There aren't many plants. Why? Because plants need light to live. Snakes and lizards live here. Jaguars like to live in this part, too!

### Forest floor
In this part, there are many insects and spiders—some spiders are as big as plates! There are many large animals. And people!

**12** **Work with a partner.**
Talk about the different parts of the rain forest.

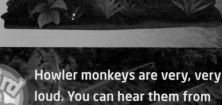

weird but true

Howler monkeys are very, very loud. You can hear them from 5 kilometers (3 miles) away.

There are gorillas in this part.

# Protect animal habitats.

Protect animal homes. Remember that we share our world with animals.

## How can we protect animal habitats?

 NATIONAL GEOGRAPHIC

**Jaguar, Yasuni National Park, Ecuador**

# What's for Dinner?

**Look and circle.**

1. He's _____.
   a. swimming   b. fishing

2. He's having _____ for dinner.
   a. fish   b. vegetables

Traditional Fishing,
Mare, New Caledonia

**1** **Listen and read.** TR: 70

**2** **Listen and say.** TR: 71

We all love food. We can find food in stores or at the market. What's your favorite food? Let's go shopping!

a bottle of oil

a jar of olives

a loaf of bread

**a box of cereal**

**a bowl of sugar**

**a glass of juice**

**a can of soda**

**a piece of cake**

**3** **Work with a partner.** Say what you see. Add on to the sentence each time. Take turns.

At the market, I see a jar of olives.

At the market, I see a jar of olives and a loaf of bread.

Are there **any** oranges?     Yes, there are **some** in the fruit bowl.
Are there **any** bananas?     No, there aren't **any.**
Is there **any** milk?     Yes, there is **some** in the fridge.
Is there **any** bread?     No, there isn't **any.**

**4** **Play a game.** Play with a partner. Spin. Ask and answer.

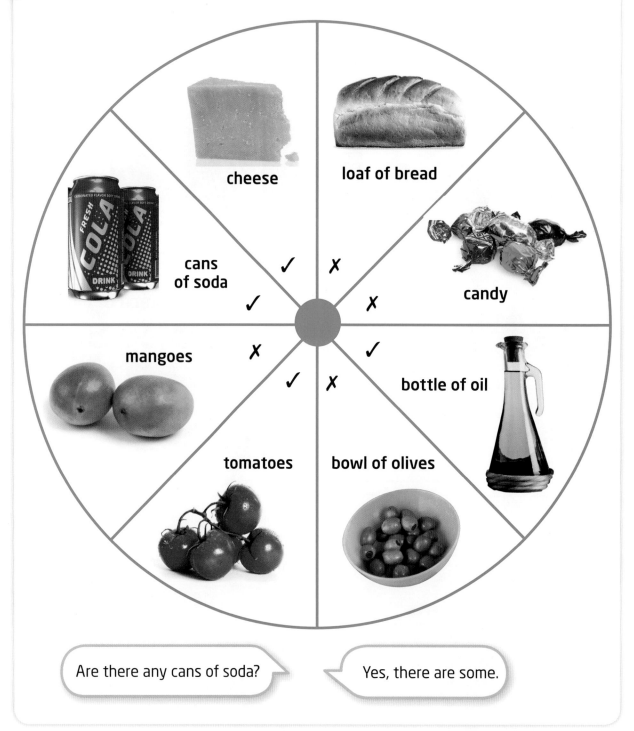

Are there any cans of soda?

Yes, there are some.

**5** **Listen and say.** Read and write. TR: 73

money

put away

a price

compare

buy

1. Which drink is better for you? Let's _____ them.

   a. buy          b. compare          c. eat

2. Can you help me _____ the food in the fridge, please?

   a. compare          b. put away          c. buy

3. The _____ of that loaf of bread is ninety cents.

   a. price          b. money          c. smell

4. Let's _____ some milk. We don't have any.

   a. compare          b. put away          c. buy

**6** **Listen and stick.** Work with a partner. TR: 74

1          2          3          4          5

| Are there any cookies? | Yes, there are **a few.** |
| Is there any orange juice? | Yes, there is **a little.** |

**7** **Read and write.**

1. Is there any ice cream? Yes, there _____.

2. Are there any grapes? Yes, there _____.

3. Is there any milk? Yes, there _____.

4. Are there any potatoes? Yes, there _____.

**8** **Play a game.** Cut out the game board and the cards on page 111. Put the cards on the board. Play with a partner.

B1. Is there any soda?

No, there isn't any soda.
A1. Are there any eggs?

Yes, there are a few. Here you are.

# Let's Go Shopping!

Let's go shopping. Let's go shopping,
let's go shopping today.
Let's go shopping to buy some food,
then go home to put it away.

A bowl of pasta, a jar of spice,
a glass of juice, and cake are nice!
Let's go now. Let's buy some food.
Let's go shopping, just me and you!

**THE SOUNDS OF ENGLISH** TR: 77

juice

**10** **Listen and say.**

1. juice        jar

2. jacket       jeans

3. giraffe      orange

## 11 **Listen and read.** TR: 78

# What I Eat

We all eat different things. The photographer Peter Menzel travels to different countries to see what people eat. These are some of his photos. They show what one person eats in one day.

Cao is 16. She's an acrobat and works in the circus. She has yogurt and fruit for breakfast. For lunch she has a bowl of rice with meat, eggs, and onions. She doesn't have dinner because she performs in a show every evening.

acrobat, China

Akbar is a bread baker. He has eggs, salad, and some tea for breakfast. He doesn't stop working for lunch. He has some snacks—a bunch of grapes, some tomatoes, and some of his bread. He has a big dinner at home. He eats meat, rice, yogurt, and some more of his bread!

Every day, half the people in the world eat rice.

baker, Iran

## 12 **Work with a partner.**

What do the people eat?
What do you eat?

Cao has yogurt for breakfast.

I do, too!

# Eat nutritious food.

Eat fresh food. Eat good food. Read the labels on boxes and cans.

What do you eat? Is your food good for you?

NATIONAL GEOGRAPHIC

Bear fishing, Brooks Falls, Alaska

**Work with a partner.** You have three minutes to answer the questions.

## One to Ten!

1. Write three forms of transportation whose name begins with S.

2. Are there any potatoes?

   Yes, there are a _____!

3. You _____ with your nose and _____ with your tongue.

4. What lives in a hive?

5. I ride my bike to school.

   I don't. I _____.

6. Why does an ostrich have long legs?

7. A _____ of cereal and a _____ of olives, please.

8. Write three things that are sweet.

9. The rabbit _____ soft.

10. How was the soup?

    It _____ delicious.

Finish

Start

12

1

11

2

Why . . . ?   Why . . . ?

Is . . . ?   What . . . ?

10

3

What . . . ?   Do . . . ?

How . . . ?   What . . . ?

9

4

Is . . . ?   Are . . . ?

Why . . . ?   How . . . ?

8

5

7   6

Tails. Why do goats have horns?

**Work with a partner.** Use a coin.
Heads = 2 spaces, Tails = 1 space.
Look. Ask and answer.

TR: 79

This is our world.
Everybody's got a song to sing.
Each boy and girl.
This is our world!

I say "our!" you say "world!"
Our!
World!
Our!
World!

I say "boy!" you say "girl!"
Boy!
Girl!
Boy!
Girl!

I say "Everybody move…"
I say "Everybody stop…"
Everybody stop!

This is our world.
Everybody's got a song to sing.
Each boy and girl.
This is our world!

Let's sing!

# Unit 1 Work TR: 16

**What does your father do?**
**What does your mother do?**
**What does your brother do?**
**What do they do?**

What does your father do?

He's a doctor. He's a doctor.
He's a doctor. Yes, he is!

I want to be a doctor!
I want to be a singer!
I want to be a rock star!
I want to be a farmer!
I want to be a dentist!
I want to be a chef!
I want to do it all!

**CHORUS**

What does your mother do?

She's a singer. She's a singer.
She's a singer. Yes, she is!

**CHORUS**

What does your brother do?

He's a teacher. He's a
    teacher.
He's a teacher. Yes, he is.

What do you like to do?
What do you want to be?
What do you want to be?
Please tell me!

I want to be a doctor!
I want to be a singer!
I want to be a rock star!
I want to be a farmer!
I want to be a dentist!
I want to be a chef!
I want to do it all!

**CHORUS**

# Unit 2 Let's Eat! TR: 24

**Let's eat!**
**Do you like chicken?**
**Let's eat!**
**Do you like bread?**
**Let's eat!**
**Are there any carrots?**
**Let's eat!**

Are there any mangoes?
Is there any cheese?
Is there any yogurt?
May I have some, please?

Yes, there are mangoes.
Yes, there is some cheese.
There isn't any yogurt.
Come and eat with me.

**CHORUS**

Is there any pasta?
Are there any beans?
Is there any meat?
May I have some, please?

Yes, there is some pasta.
Yes, there are beans.
There isn't any meat.
Please, come and eat
    with me.

**CHORUS**

I like chicken.
And you like beans.
Let's make a soup!

**CHORUS**

Let's eat!

## Unit 3 Taking Care TR: 32

**I love taking care of my pets.**
**I love taking care of my family.**
**I love taking care of them all.**
**I'm happy that there are so many!**

I love taking care of my pets.
I love to pick them up, and hug them, too.
But before I get to play with my pets,
I have some work to do.

I have to comb my cat, feed my dog,
protect my bird, and pick up my frog.
I have to wash my goat, brush my horse,
and I can't forget to bathe my snake, of
   course.

**CHORUS**

I love taking care of my family.
I love to hug them, too.

But before I get to play with my family,
I have some work to do.

I have to read to my sister,
take care of my brothers,
and hold hands with my grandmother.
I have to teach my brothers their 1, 2, 3's
and carry my family's new baby.

I love taking care of my pets.
I love taking care of my family.
After all my work is done,
I get to have some fun with my...
cat and dog, bird and frog,
goat and horse, and my snake, of course!
My sisters and my brothers, my grandmother,
and even my family's new baby!

## Unit 4 A Great New Town TR: 41

Can I help you? You look lost.
Can I help you find your way?
Can I help you? You look lost.
Can I help you today?

**I'm new in town. I think**
**   I'm lost.**
**Can you help me find my**
**   way?**
**I'm new in town.**
**Can you help me with my**
**   busy day?**

Where are the post office,
   the toy store,
the supermarket, and the
   park?

Where's the bakery?
Where's the library?

Where are the zoo, the
   school, and a
swimming pool?

**CHORUS**

I can help you. You're not
   lost.
I can help you find your way.
I can help you. You're not lost.
I can help you today.

Here's the post office,

the toy store, the
   supermarket,
and the park.
Here's the bakery, the
   library, the zoo,
the school, a swimming pool,
and a movie theater, too!

I can help you. You're not
   lost.
I can help you today.
I can help you find your
   way, and you'll be OK,
in your great new town
   today!

Thank you for helping me
   to find my way.
Thank you for helping me
   with my busy day,
in my great new town
   today!
In my great new town
   today!

## Unit 5 How Do You Get to School?

**How do you get to school?**
**How do you get to school?**
**How do you get to school?**
**How do you get to school?**

I take the bus to school.
I do, too.
I ride my bike to school.
I do, too.

### CHORUS

My mom drives me to school.
My mom does, too.
I coast downhill to school.
I do, too.

### CHORUS

Listen and I'll tell you
Listen and I'll tell you
Listen and I'll tell you
how I get to school.

I take a ferry to school. Yes, I do.
I take a ferry to school. Do you
    take one, too?

I take the subway to school.
    Yes, I do.
I take the subway to school.
    Do you take it, too?

### CHORUS

## Unit 6 Our Senses TR: 59

How does the cake taste?
It tastes sweet.
How does a kitten feel?
It feels soft.

**Let's count our senses, 1, 2, 3, 4, 5!**
**Listen.**
**Look.**
**Feel.**
**Taste.**
**Smell.**
**It's great to be alive!**

How does the drum sound?
It sounds loud.

How does a flower smell?
It smells good.

### CHORUS

How does the garden look?
It looks beautiful.
How does a hug feel?
It feels great!

### CHORUS

## Unit 7 **Why? Because!** TR: 67

Why does a giraffe have a long, long neck?
Why?
Why?
Because it eats leaves at the tops of the trees.

**I want to know why.**
**I want to know why.**
**Why?**
**Because I want to know why!**

Why does a frog have strong legs?
Why?
Why?
Because it hops, swims, and jumps.

**CHORUS**

Animals are amazing.
They do so many things.
And I have just one thing to say.
Why?

Why does a polar bear have white fur?
Why?
Why?
Because it lives in ice and snow.

**CHORUS**

## Unit 8 **Let's Go Shopping!** TR: 76

**Let's go shopping. Let's go shopping,**
**let's go shopping today.**
**Let's go shopping to buy some food,**
**then go home to put it away.**

A jar of jelly is no fun,
if there isn't any bread to spread it on.
A bowl of rice is very nice,
but it tastes better with some spice.

**CHORUS**

Let's buy some pasta at the shop,
and some sauce to put on top.
Let's buy a cake. Cake's a treat.
I like cake because it's sweet!

A bowl of pasta, a jar of spice,
a glass of milk, and cake are nice!
Let's go now. Let's buy some food.
Let's go shopping, just me and you!

**CHORUS**

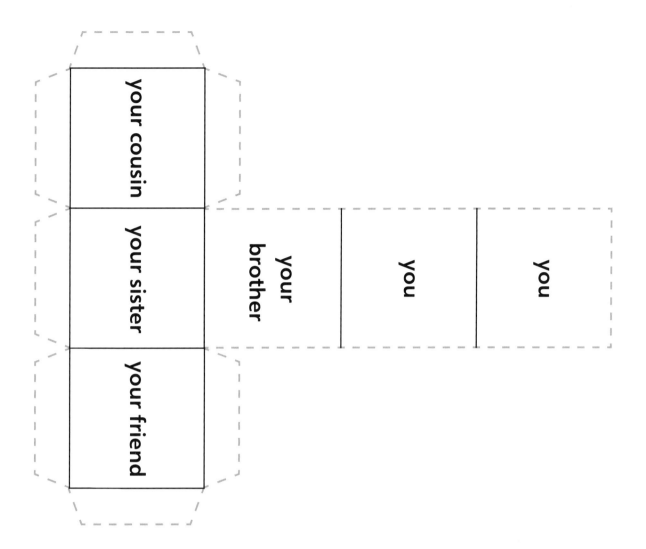

your cousin

your sister

your friend

your brother

you

you

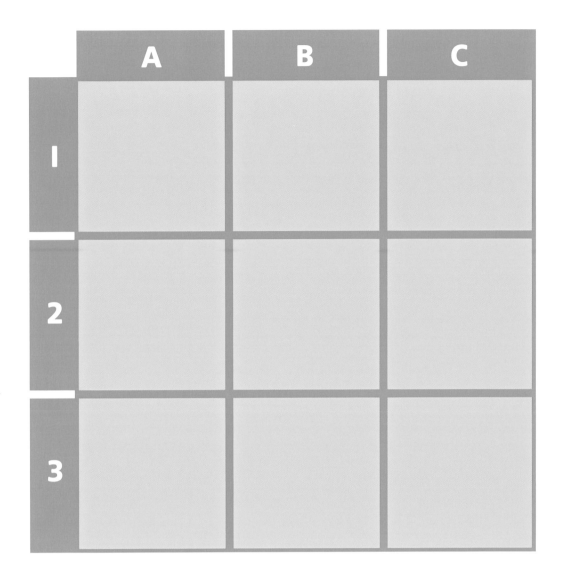

**1** do my homework
in the evening

the same?

**2** eat lunch
at 12:00

the same?

**3** wash my face
in the evening

the same?

**5** have a snack
after school

the same?

**4** brush my teeth
after breakfast

the same?

**6** ride my bike
on Saturdays

the same?

**7** watch TV

the same?

**8** make my bed
in the morning

the same?

never

never

sometimes

sometimes

usually

usually

always

always

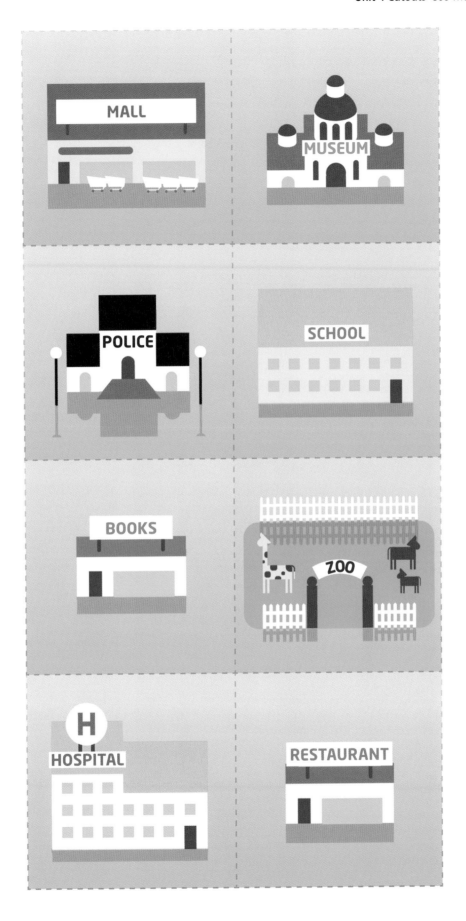

Jenny

to school

Sam

to school

Jenny
likes

for breakfast

Sam
likes

for breakfast

Jenny

wants to

Sam

wants to

Jenny

at 9:00 p.m.

Sam

at 9:00 p.m.

Jenny

on Saturdays

Sam

on Saturdays

Jenny

likes to

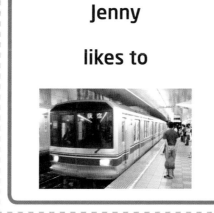

Sam

likes to

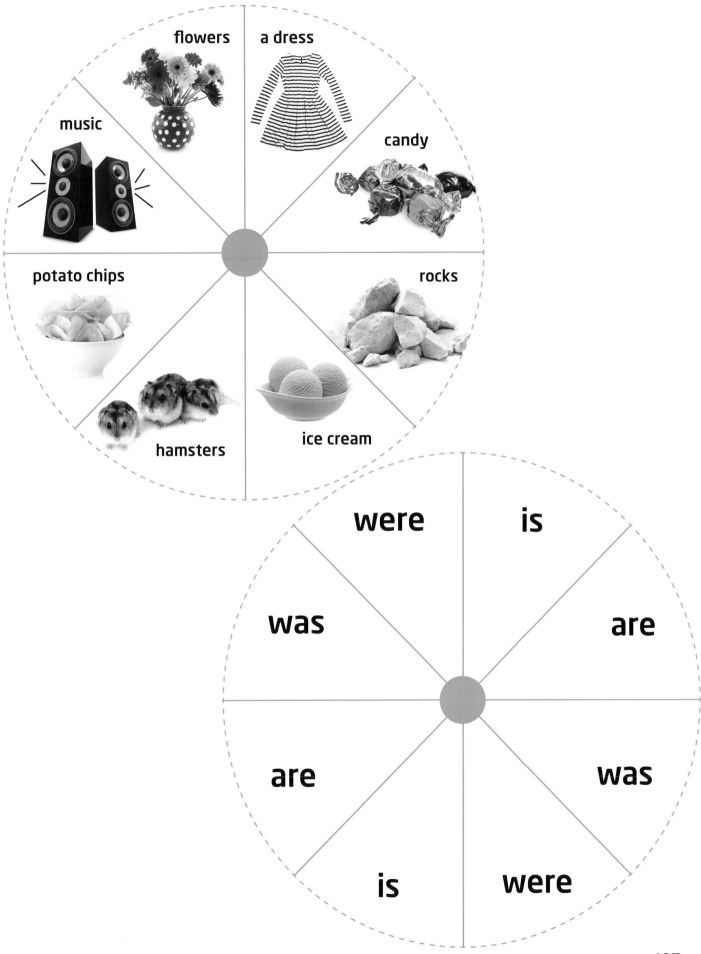

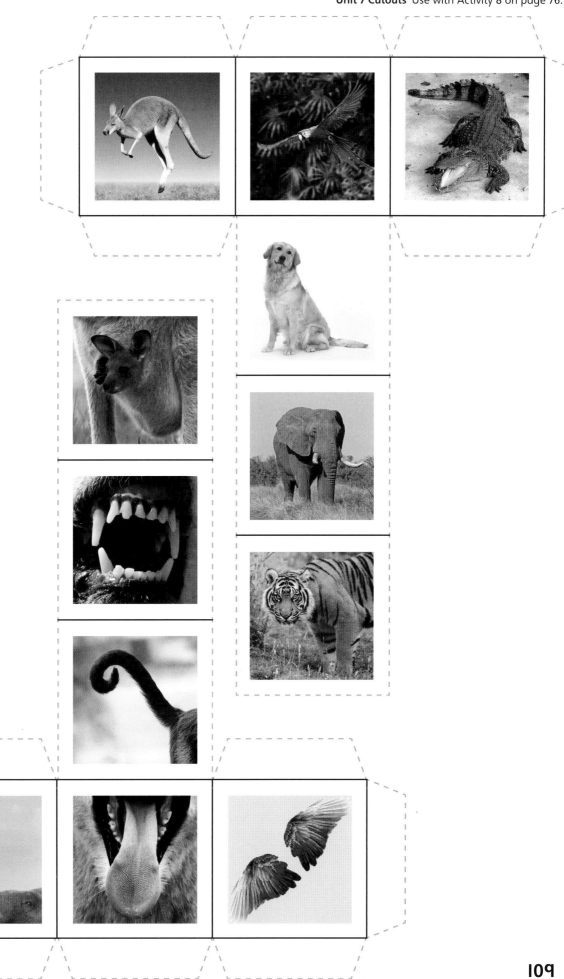

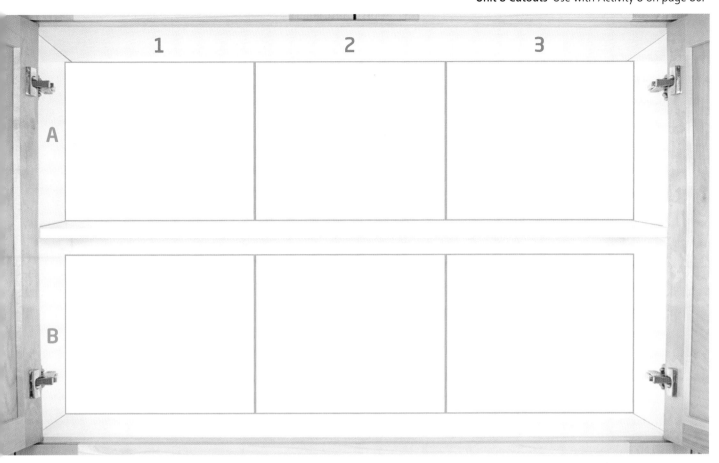

III